To Be, Conjugated

poems by brian koukol

Contents

Public Charge

The stunted, blunted surface
of my crumpled, crippled shell
tells a story misremembered
in a tongue you cannot speak
of glass once sharp and vital
thought softened by the sea

But salt and sand don't dull the honed
so much as to prove the fact
that we discarded bottles
turn gem through agitation

You pick us up,
you put us down,
you feed us to the dunes

Cast aside like garbage,
but like garbage, we refuse.

The Consonance and Dissonance of Decrepitude

If every sleep be a little death
then my resurrection machine is broken,
for I wake each morning
a weaker version of the one who came before.

A layer here, a layer there,
in thinnest parchment sloughed away,
my words and deeds and hopes in reams
do lift and fly and fray.

But between those times of yet and gone,
my breath does light the vacuum black
and birth a cosmos all its own
while I spit galaxies in my dreams.

(n)evergreen

in the time of crushing crushes
my hands had better things to do
then pine for others to hold them
knowing without knowing
that small hands are more sensitive
and what they feel most is pain
for what are pines without their needles
but grotesque, unfit, and scorned?

now I am a bristlecone
my bark is set, my trunk is twisted
and a lonely hiker finds me beautiful
but my hands are gnarled claws
that scratch when they kiss skin
and time has contorted those fingertips
into barbs that hook themselves;
to touch now is to be touched
where the nerves are loathe to feel
beneath those calluses of burl.

Diagenesis

I see my evolution sketched in pencil—
less *The March of Progress*
than the march of progression
toward muscle cells
that ideate
and gesture
and attempt
and succeed.

I see my debilitation in the layers of my armrest—
like flakes of of human clay
muddied into fragile shale—
from the dog-dayed romance of
naugahyde and short-sleeved skin
to the stone-cold shoulder of
a chronic winter coat;
the inexorable slide of limb toward precipice
stymied by a handful of rubber bands,
a wrap of tacky elastic bandage,
a spiral of hockey tape,
a fleeced lamb.
But still that petrified little arm
ideated
and gestured
and attempted
and finally fell for good.

Anachronism

They say to be mindful,
to live in the present,
but the present is a Greek gift
stuffed with endless suffering
to be avoided at all costs.

Living in the moment means
starving for air when the ventilator comes off,
mindful of a nearly sprung mortal coil through
transfers, meals, and breathless dumps.

You only live once,
but that once feels nearly done
when the pain of spinal disintegration
strangles hearing into waves of agony
modulated by the beating of a heart
prone to wander and pause and prematurely contract.

The true beauty lies in escaping the moment,
swaddled by the daughter of the wind
and the son of the morning star
in a curated past of safety and warmth
or a future of hope and possibility.

Denial is a river of abstraction
that salves the feet of the weary,
but a present that dams and diverts
stymies with blisters and malaise.

The moment means misery.
The moment means pain.
The moment means chains till you die.
You can keep your moment—
I'll take anything but,
where I can breathe again.

A Painted Smile, Chipped

I was born a virtual adoptee,
handed to biological parents
who could love, but never understand —
and me, wailing:
wearing kidskin over sawdust,
the bisque of my blushing face already hardening
into inspirational, resilient precociousness.
In pursuit of acceptance,
I became a human doll
and the world knew how to define me.
But dolls and precociousness are both outgrown —
exposing the hollow beneath the mohair wig
that turned those blushing cheeks
red with the rage
of a me who never was
and now too late to start.

Take a Penny, Give a Penny

all relationships involving caregiving fail
an able-bodied man once said
but when failure is not an option
what holds two bodies together
beyond their expiration date
when dysfunction wounds and cuts
but can't outpace the love
that once burned with ardor
and now burns with obligation

if glue is made from picked-over bones
our bond will never break
forged by a shared and lengthy past
and the habit of joint survival
but chronic heat gone cold can crack
and therein we rediscover our passion
fishing in the fissures to catch
that tangerine room we shared
in our own bungalow haven
before our selfless dreams
atrophied alongside my muscles

true romance is give and take
though even the truest
can't live so lopsided as
a pillar of equity
unbuttressed by equality

take a penny
give a penny
but all of mine are green

They Call Me Wheelchair-bound

They, meaning those not damned to life
as an intractable husk,
incapable of effective movement,
shackled by a conspiracy of gravity and
wasted muscle
not to a deathbed, but a dyingbed;
forever fading, detaching, yearning.

They, meaning those ignorant typicals
who misconstrue
the greatest emancipator since Lincoln
as a pitiable device
that binds, confines, sidelines.

They, meaning those who count
themselves
awake when their eyes part,
rather than when their wheelchair starts,
the click of its twin motors crying
liberty, equality, fraternity
to the tyrant immobility.

They, meaning those unable
to fathom the miraculous joys
of moving, of interacting, of existing
in this shared reality
when atrophy and entropy demand otherwise.

They, meaning those who may yet get their epiphany,
when thoughtless chain-smoking leads to mortal
Cheyne-Stoking
and they sprawl on their dyingbed,
yearning for wheels.

Fear of a Spark

I met someone new today—
not a doctor
or a caregiver,
but a person unversed in the toll
of decay and disease and death.

She danced in exuberant joy,
not because she'd finally broken down
and taken an unfairly maligned opiate,
but because she'd bought
a new pair of tights
that were the best thing ever.

As she kicked and strutted and whooped,
I longed for a shell to retreat into:
deep and dark and still—
a place not of sparks
but of embers.

Feeding Time

You tried to feed me a bite of lunch,
but my jaw wouldn't open to accommodate;
when you tugged on my lips to force a fit,
invalidity realized overtook my mind
and I backed away my wheelchair
to escape my inescapable fate,
though you followed me, shoving—
the toasted wheat cutting corners
of both mouth and self-respect
like lemon on an un-scabbed wound.
Forcibly fellated by a BLTA sandwich,
I twisted and turned and wrenched myself free,
my tongue resisting admittance.
"Don't spit that on the floor," you warned,
but my id needed it out and at once.
You raved and you cursed,
threatened to leave me
unfed, undead,
(in a limbo between in- and -dependent)
despite the unheard explanations
of a knee-jerk, post-traumatized brain.
When you have none, agency supplants even dignity:
to starve, to eat, both what and how
is a choice almost all can make
for that elusive, illusive control.
Eating disorders dig deep, dark defense
that hurt the self most of all
when pain is the only way to exorcise

the guilt of needing, and taking, and consuming.
[Remember when I called my mom a cunt
because she reheated my chicken marsala
with barbecue sauce by mistake?]
I'd kill myself, but suicide is impossible,
and my last taste must never be surrender.

Necromancy for the Bitter

I planted a coast live oak seedling
in the front yard today,
not with my own vestigial hands,
but through the sentinel, pallbearing palms
of an able-bodied surrogate.

I can see it now, six inches tall and
stolid against the gentle breeze—
a pittance of cupped, spiny-toothed
leaves dangling from a stem curved in
proud contrast to my corrected scoliosis.

Long after my ventilator is sent to palliate
another among the unfortunate dying
and my lungs are but dust
on a slagged pair of Harrington rods,
the little oak might be a three-foot whip,
battered but not broken by the ephemeral desert breath
that creeps over mountains named by the Spanish for
some saint that never kept their end of the deal.

If drought holds off for a year or three
and my oak escapes the quirks of fate,
one day it might spread and thrive
until its carpet of jagged leaves bloody
the bare feet of a child or passing Pomeranian
and I live again through their pain.

Fear of the Common Cold

It's in the air, it's on the walls,
on your hands, the doorknob, the dog.
I try to quarantine myself
to keep the killer at bay—
and killer it is, thanks to muscular dystrophy
(my mistress of morbidities),
where sniffles become
bronchitis become
pneumonia become
white lilies and a slew
of guiltily relieved family members—
but I need total care
to exist from day-to-day
and you can't wash your hands fast enough
to offset their constant wanderings.
I can't run, I can't hide;
it's probably already inside me,
biding its time and itching for mine
until a snuffed pinch of my remains
(engraved but not interred
in a silver pendant of willows weeping)
disappears forgotten into a drawer.
Until then, all I can do is sit fast,
facing my fate with a stone stoicism
and a steady supply of zinc
clutched like a lucky rabbit's foot
in a trench at Passchendaele,

where muddy mucus hisses
for the snake oil of deliverance.
There, inside my throat—
a dry patch, a tickle, a dirge.
Is it to be life, or death?
Only tomorrow will tell.
I gaze into the abyss,
braver than you know.

On the Paradox of Finity

In the movies, terminal illness is
nothing but a prop in an able-bodied psalm
about living life to the fullest, but
those doing the actual dying soon learn
that as the body fades and the world shrinks,
the days bleed together until exsanguinated
and embalmed by a time not short
but endless—turned circles that burn away hours
as ephemeral as a dwindling attention span
in a false purgatory of repetition
and routine that teases of immortality
but stinks of a manic boredom stretching
seconds to eons and gone much too fast.
With too little time to do big things,
little withers to nothing at all,
like a nearly-empty bottle of hand soap
stretched by the tap until worthless.

Mandatory Minimum

I wanted to tell that codger who cornered us
between the box crackers and shelf-stable cheese
that I brought something to the table too
when he told me I was lucky to have you,
recalling the snap of gentle fury conducted
straight to my psyche by your helping hands
when those sleep-deprived, weaponized sighs
burp festering, acidic resentment at the
continued existence of this life-sucking
incubus who turns every vanity mirror into
the back of a spoon, revealing one grotesque
truth beneath that moon-faced mask:
eggshells which could be walked by gentle feet
are crushed beneath the weight of churning tires.

Slings and Arrows

I thrust my head from the back of the sling
at the accusation that I don't care about your pain,
letting gravity rip at my upper trapezius
while you wheel me suspended toward the blessed
doorway:

as if a mid-day bowel movement were a red line
crossed,

as if my mere existence were an affront of my own
making
and not a conspiracy of careless ejaculate and a faulty X
chromosome,

as if i'd asked to be in this world, in this body
that takes and takes and knows it,
like a glutton hungry for best selves,

as if I can hurt myself enough with a stretch toward the
jamb
to salve your agonies and apologize
for the selfishness, once removed
that I balance, once removed.

Make Way

Separate but meekful, I acquiesce
to the touch of the gloved hand,
as if crippled skin were unclean by nature—
a poison whose only antidote is quarantine
and the violence of powder-free nitrile.

Shunned into a life of parallel solitude,
I take my society in the fronds
of a bathroom bamboo palm,
surprisingly turgid despite my caress.
Neither do my terrier's paws shrink
away in terror as they traipse across
my abdomen in the dead of night.
And what of the closeted jackets
I insinuate my face among,
indulging in forbidden textures and scents
while unbarred by superstition?
The moths don't consume them,
no seams are rent, but I pay in jealousy:
greening as they hang tightly together
while I'm left to hang separately,
drifting alone in a two-person boat.

Unicornered

A pastel sweatshirt with a screen-printed unicorn
cornered me outside the poke bowl spot
and asked if it could lay hands on me
on behalf of its human host
who may have been a time traveler
with her white slouch socks and Keds
and a sidekick in full Goth regalia.
They were two sides of a coin
or perhaps a communion wafer,
dry and alienating at first bite
but soon to sweeten when chewed.

Superfluity

Like mewling puppies, we piled for warmth
through those young winters of contentment,
arranged not as spoons but sharp forks,
our tines running out in collusion.

Then a ventilator came to keep me abreath
though it dried up my raison d'etre
when our delicate alloy eroded beneath
a frigid mist of pressurized spittle.

Now we lie together
like mismatched cutlery —
you, a spork, perhaps:
doing the work of two
half as well as either;
and me, a knife of silver gilt,
and all that that entails.

Lebensunwertes Leben

Is dolphin worth less than orange roughy,
because dolphin lives one fifth as long?
Some sponges live centuries longer than either;
should sponges inherit the Earth?

A cicada lives three times your mastiff,
though it spends that time sleeping in dirt.
If instead it were there to give snuggles,
would you bury poor Rex in the yard?

If a pearl oyster outlives its luster,
if you've stripped from it all that you can,
do you wear that fair necklace and flaunt it,
while you chuck those spent oysters in the surf?

Who are you to decide on its value?
Who are you to stamp life unworthy of life?
See, every story's a blink, no matter its length,
for, godless, the void is eternal.

The Truth

I hold my diarrhea for fourteen hours
before finally asking for help getting on the toilet
because I know that
the pleasure of evacuated bowels
comes at another's expense—
like how dog heaven
is also squirrel hell.

After I finish,
you crank me up in the lift,
but the sling spreads my cheeks
and I mist the seat in aerosolized shit.
While you clean it up,
I take great pains to thank you
because I know you've been feeling underappreciated
lately.

You put me in bed and roll me on my side,
holding me in place to relax my back.
A Bryan Adams song plays on the radio.

Your nose is six inches from my ass
when the new position activates my guts.
"Fart!" I warn too late.
You recoil, gagging beneath the stench of
burnt erasers and summertime roadkill
while Bryan Adams crows about heaven.

Washingtonia robusta

I am a palm tree ill at ease,
bending and bending and
knowing that one day
I will break in the wind.

And it blows.

Still Here

The pity of relations bereft at the
thought of a loved one dying before
his time dropped like lies as they
collapsed into their graves, leaving me
to pick up pieces I'd never been
expected to reassemble.

Like a mayfly long into October,
I'd outlived my expiration date,
buzzing into an autumn morning
like milk resurrected as yogurt
while those who'd grieved my loss
several times over coughed their way
into caskets and earned their place
among the procession of cardboard
boxes waylaid by procrastination.

As the get-togethers quiet and the
memories sink into the stone tablets
of nostalgia, the cold loneliness
of death may have caught up after all,
abandoning me to the icy comfort
of my own eternal company.

Diaphragm

If love lingers in the heart,
then guilt lies in the diaphragm,
knotted with ableism internalized
and weakened by its strength.

Every mess I make,
all the pants I shit,
every bed I wet,
must be vetted for self-compassion
and savored for self-hate;
for each need and want and idiosyncrasy
is ammunition for the self-inflicted,
brass casings stiffening into uselessness
that double-domed muscle which,
when pliant,
coughs free from static atelectasis
and flexes its privilege of profligacy.

Leaves

From fragile seeds we grew together,
finding comfort in our shadows.
But to bloom, I learned, one first must bolt,
so I let you damn our hallows.

And when that blossom needed room,
you pulled your roots and moved them.
Still in sight, but out of reach,
your shadow picked up with you.

Without your shade, the sun did burn—
you left me limp and weeping.
I tried to bolt in my own turn,
but found my bloom withholding.

You grew into a gardener,
though chained you were to me.
And when you tried to clear my weeds,
it left me stripped of…

To Be, Conjugated

As a teenager, I lusted in peace,
certain that no lover would ever
see a future in me,
and thus never a present;
I lived in the past tense,
stinking like a tombstone
in the springtime.

And when that lust fell to pragmatism,
I sought only a touch,
a hug, an accidental caress,
though such fancies soon crumbled
beneath the hobbling weight of
neuropathic allodynia and
a general lack of practice.

Now, all I want is eye contact
and a single soul
more happy I'm alive
than sad when I'm gone.

I'd rather suffer in something
then vanish into nothing,
though that may be where I
finally find my use as a human being,
when from my rot might spring forth a stalk
of telegraph weed, gravely transmitting
for all the universe to hear

these persistent whispers of:
I was,
I am,
I will be.

About the Writer

Raised in the suburbs of Los Angeles, Brian Koukol now makes his home among the salt breezes and open spaces of California's Central Coast, where he somehow finds time to write between soaking up the rays and eating his weight in avocados. This collection—like all of his poetry, prose, and screenwriting—is written with voice recognition and eye gaze technology on account of his lifelong nemesis, muscular dystrophy.

Visit his website at www.briankoukol.com

Independent authors feed on reviews. If you enjoyed this book, why not spend a few minutes sharing that fact with the world?

Acknowledgments

"They Call Me Wheelchair-bound" originally appeared in Wordgathering, March 2019

"(n)evergreen" originally appeared in Rogue Agent, August 2019

Excerpts of "Take a Penny, Give a Penny" and "Feeding Time" appeared in Wordgathering, September 2019

"Diagenesis" originally appeared in Wordgathering, December 2019

"Fear of a Spark" originally appeared in Wordgathering, March 2020

"Make Way" and "Lebensunwertes Leben" originally appeared in Wordgathering, September 2020

www.ingramcontent.com/pod-product-compliance
Lightning Source LLC
Chambersburg PA
CBHW051501140726
47987CB00006B/2823